LOONY GOOD CLEAN JOKES

FOR KIDS!

Bob Phillips

Illustrations by
Norm Daniels

HARVEST HOUSE PUBLISHERS
Eugene, Oregon 97402

LOONY GOOD CLEAN JOKES FOR KIDS

Copyright © 1993 by Harvest House Publishers
Eugene, Oregon 97402

Library of Congress Cataloging-in-Publication Data

Phillips, Bob, 1940-
    Loony good clean jokes for kids / Bob Phillips.
       p. m.
     ISBN 1-56507-178-6
     1. Wit and humor, Juvenile. [1. Jokes. 2. Riddles.] I. Title.
PN6163.P483   1994   93-23529
818'.5402—dc20   CIP
                                              AC

Printed in the United States of America.

94 95 96 97 98 99 00 01 — 10 9 8 7 6 5 4 3 2 1

*To the
lively, likable, loony
Lilley family.*

Contents

Light-headed Loonies

What do you have when 134 strawberries try to get through the same door?
A strawberry jam.

•

What do you get if you cross a dentist with the Tooth Fairy?
A mouthful of quarters.

•

What do you call mail sent to a cat?
Kitty letter.

•

What is gray and spins around and around?
A hippo stuck in a revolving door.

•

What do you call a hitchhiking elephant?
A two-and-a-half-ton pickup.

•

What do you get if you cross a rhinoceros and a goose?
An animal that honks before it runs you over.

•

What did the rabbits do after they got married?
Went on their bunnymoon.

•

What invention allows people to walk through walls?
Doors.

•

What do you call 500 Indians without any apples?
The Indian apple-less 500.

•

What does a tuba call his father?
Oompah-pah.

•

What is the difference between a jeweler and a jailer?
One sells watches, while the other watches cells.

•

What do you call an ice cream man in the state of Arizona?
The Good Yuma man.

•

What has a foot at each end and a foot in the middle?
A yardstick.

•

What do you get if you light a duck's tail?
A firequacker.

•

What kind of dress do you have, but never wear?
Your address.

•

What do diets and promises have in common?
They are always being broken.

•

What should you do if you accidentally eat some micro-
film?
Wait and see what develops.

•

What is black, likes peanuts, and weighs two tons?
A chocolate-covered elephant.

•

What do you call a singer who is not old enough to be a
  tenor?
A niner!

•

What is black and white and red on Christmas Eve?
Rudolph the Red-Nosed Penguin.

•

What weighs three tons, has tusks, and loves pepperoni
  pizza?
An Italian circus elephant.

•

What is the difference between an excited skunk and a
  calm skunk?
An $80 laundry bill.

•

What time is it when an elephant climbs into your bed?
Time to get a new bed.

•

What is the difference between a man going up the stairs
  and a man looking up the stairs?
One steps up the stairs, and the other stares up the steps.

•

What kind of music do welders dance to?
Heavy metal.

Lively
Loonies

What is harder than cutting school?
Gluing it back together.

•

What happens when frogs get married?
They live hoppily ever after.

•

What is the skunk's motto?
Walk softly and carry a big stink.

•

What is a rabbit's favorite song?
Hoppy Birthday.

•

What kind of duck robs banks?
A safe quacker.

•

What is purple and crazy?
A grape nut.

•

In what kind of stroller do you wheel an infant insect?
A baby buggy.

What is the difference between a chocolate chip cookie
and an elephant?
You can't dunk an elephant in your milk.

•

What do you get when you chop down a tuna tree?
Fish sticks.

•

What is pronounced like one letter, written with three
letters, and belongs to all animals?
Eye.

•

What is the wife of a jeweler called?
Ruby.

•

What does a tiger do when it rains?
It gets wet.

•

What did the prisoner say when he bumped into the
  governor?
Pardon me!

What is orange, runs on batteries, and costs 6 million
  dollars?
The Bionic Carrot.

•

What is beautiful, gray, and wears glass slippers?
Cinderelephant.

•

What is black and white and hides in caves?
A zebra who owes money.

•

What city is named after a small stone?
Little Rock, Arkansas.

•

What rolls in the mud and plays trick-or-treat?
The Halloween Pig.

•

What has seeds, a stem, and swings from tree to tree?
Tarzan, King of the Grapes.

•

What is large and gray and bumps into submarines?
A near-sighted hippo scuba diver.

•

What does a slice of toast wear to bed?
Jam-mies.

•

What cheese can't stop talking?
Chatter cheese.

•

What piece of furniture will never learn to swim?
The sink.

•

What do you get when you cross a black dog and a white
dog?
A greyhound.

•

What is the snootiest dog?
A cocky spaniel.

3

Lana & Lark
Loony

Lana: Where would you send a man to get an appetite?
Lark: I have no clue.
Lana: To Hungary.

•

Lana: How many Teamsters does it take to load a truck?
Lark: I don't know.
Lana: Fourteen. You got a problem with that?

•

Lana: How many loony terrorists does it take to screw in
a light bulb?
Lark: I can't guess.
Lana: One hundred. One to screw it in and 99 to hold the
house hostage.

•

Lana: What is the difference between a rooster, Uncle
Sam, and a loony old maid?
Lark: I have no idea.
Lana: The rooster says, "Cock-a-doodle-doo"; Uncle
Sam says, "Yankee-doodle-doo"; and a loony old maid
says, "Any dude'll do."

•

Lana: How many people does it take to clean up a hazardous waste dump?
Lark: You tell me.
Lana: Fifty. One tractor driver and 49 loony lawyers.

Lana: How many members of the Loony family does it take to screw in a light bulb?
Lark: What's a light bulb?

•

Lana: How did the father flea get home for Christmas?
Lark: I give up.
Lana: By Greyhound.

•

Lana: What is the difference between the rising sun and
the setting sun?
Lark: Who knows?
Lana: All the difference in the world.

•

Lana: How many loony mothers does it take to screw in a
light bulb?
Lark: You've got me.
Lana: None. It's all right; I'll just sit here in the dark.

•

Lana: What is black and white and black and white?
Lark: My mind is a blank.
Lana: A penguin tumbling down an iceberg.

•

Lana: How intelligent is your loony pet duck?
Lark: That's a mystery.
Lana: Very intelligent! I'll prove it by having him make a
few wisequacks.

•

Lana: Who killed a fourth of all the people in the world?
Lark: I'm blank.
Lana: Cain, when he killed Abel.

•

Lana: If a king sits on gold, who sits on silver?
Lark: I don't have the foggiest.
Lana: The Lone Ranger.

•

Lana: There is a donkey on one side of a deep river, and a bundle of hay on the other side. How can the donkey get the hay? There is no bridge, and he cannot swim. Do you give up?

Lark: Yes, I give up.

Lana: So did the other donkey.

•

Lana: How many doctors does it take to examine an elephant?

Lark: It's unknown to me.

Lana: It depends on whether or not the elephant has health insurance.

4

Laughable Loonies

My loony town is so small that the local gangland boss, Mr. Big, is a midget.

•

My loony boss has a heart of stone. He can even trace his roots back to a petrified forest.

•

My loony secretary isn't an office gossip. She's a magician. She can turn an eyeful or an earful into a mouthful.

•

I'm not sure it's true, but I heard that in Loonyville they hang spaghetti on Christmas trees instead of tinsel. The only problem is the meatballs don't light up.

•

Loony hostess: You know, I've heard a great deal about you.
Loony politician: Possibly, but you can't prove a thing.

•

Loony mom: For dessert, you have your choice of good or evil.

Loony Lyle: What do you mean?

Loony mom: Angel food cake or devil's food cake.

•

Loony wife: Wake up! Wake up! There's a burglar in the kitchen, and he's eating the leftover stew we had for supper.

Loony husband: Go back to sleep and don't worry, dear. I'll bury him in the morning.

•

Last night I slept like a loony lawyer. First I lied on one side, then I lied on the other.

•

An angry loony worker went into her company's payroll office to complain that her paycheck was $50 short.

The payroll supervisor checked the books and said, "I see here that last week you were overpaid by $50. I can't recall your complaining about that."

"Well, I'm willing to overlook an occasional error, but this is two in a row," said the loony worker.

•

"I really loved my vacation in California," said the loony lady on the plane to the man sitting next to her.

"Where did you stay?" he asked.

"San Jose."

"Madam, in California we pronounce the *J* as an *H*. We say San Hosay. How long were you there?"

"All of Hune and most of Huly."

•

If your aunt had an upset stomach, what would you call her?
Antacid.

•

What would you get if you crossed poison ivy and a four-leaf clover?
A rash of good luck.

•

You peel the outside, boil the inside, nibble on the outside, and throw the inside into the garbage. What is it?
Corn on the cob.

•

If your brother had a split personality, who would he be?
Your half brother.

•

If your aunt ran off to get married, what would you call her?
Antelope.

•

Loony customer: Does the manager know you knocked over this whole pile of canned tomatoes?
Loony stock boy: I think so. He's underneath.

•

Once upon a time there was a loony ventriloquist who was so bad, you could see his lips move even when he wasn't saying anything.

•

Did you hear about the loony fishhook with a camera on it? It was invented to take pictures of the fish that got away.

•

If Fortune had a daughter, what would she be called? *Miss Fortune.*

•

A zebra with wide stripes married a zebra with narrow stripes. Their first son had no stripes. What did they call him? *Leroy.*

•

If you saw nine elephants walking down the street with red socks and one elephant walking down the street with green socks, what would this prove? *That nine out of ten elephants wear red socks.*

•

Loony mother: Leslie, will you help me fix dinner?
Loony Leslie: I didn't know it was broken.

•

Loony boy: They call a man's wife his better half, don't
   they?
Loony father: Yes, they do.
Loony boy: Then I guess if a man marries twice, there's
   nothing left of him.

•

Loony Lenora: Did you hear about the man who bought
   a new pair of snow tires?
Loony Leonard: No, what happened?
Loony Lenora: They melted before he got home.

5

Loony Legacy

My business is for the birds, said the loony pet store owner.

•

Loony Leonard: You wouldn't hit a man with glasses, would you?
Loony bully: No way! I always use my fists.

•

Loony son: I'm really glad you named me Larry.
Loony mother: Why?
Loony son: That's what all the kids at school call me.

•

Loony teacher: If you took three apples from a basket that contained 13 apples, how many apples would you have?
Loony student: If you took three apples, you'd have three apples.

•

Did you hear about the loony shirts and blouses with boards sewn into the seams? They are for people with poor posture.

•

Did you hear about the loony gift-wrapped empty boxes? They are to give as presents to people who say, "I don't need anything."

•

Loony passenger: Does this airplane fly faster than sound?
Loony flight attendant: It certainly does.
Loony passenger: Then would you ask the pilot to slow down? My friend and I would like to talk.

•

Loony employer: And you say you've been fired from ten different jobs?
Loony worker: Well, my father always said, "Never be a quitter!"

•

Can giraffes have babies?
No, they can only have giraffes.

•

Loony speaker: A horrible thing has happened. I've just lost my wallet with $500 in it. I'll give $50 to anyone who will return it.
Loony voice from the rear: I'll give $100.

•

An elderly woman was sitting on a plane and getting increasingly nervous about the thunderstorm raging outside. She turned to a minister who was sitting next to her: "Reverend, you are a man of God. Why can't you do something about this problem?"

The loony minister replied: "Lady, I'm in sales, not management."

The loony doctor opened the window wide. He said to me, "Stick your tongue out the window."

I said, "What for?"

He said, "I'm mad at my neighbors."

•

Loony boss: You are recommending Jack for a raise? I can't believe it—he's the laziest worker on the line!

Loony foreman: Yes, but his snoring keeps the other workers awake!

•

Four-year-old Loony Lucy was visiting her grandparents.
When she was put to bed, she sobbed and said she was
afraid of the dark and wanted to go home.

"But you don't sleep with the light on at home, do you,
darling?" asked her grandmother.

"No," replied Loony Lucy, "but there it's my own dark."

•

Loony Lupie: Why is daddy singing so much tonight?

Loony mother: He's trying to sing the baby to sleep
before the babysitter gets here.

Loony Lupie: You know, if I were the baby, I'd pretend I
was asleep.

•

I have a very fine loony doctor. If you can't afford the
operation, he touches up the X rays.

•

I went to visit a doctor about my sore foot. He said, "I'll
have you walking in an hour." He did. He stole my car.

•

Did you hear about the loony speech school? They teach
you how to speak clearly. To do this they fill your
mouth with marbles. You are supposed to talk clearly
right through the marbles. Every day you lose one
marble. When you've lost all your marbles ... you're
done.

•

Who said, "Will you please join me?"
A person who was coming apart.

6

Leonard & Leona Loony

Leonard: What does the lighthouse keeper play in the village orchestra?
Leona: I can't guess.
Leonard: The foghorn.

•

Leonard: What do you serve when an oat comes to dinner?
Leona: I have no idea.
Leonard: Oatmeal.

•

Leonard: What is the oldest form of social security?
Leona: You tell me.
Leonard: Suspenders.

•

Leonard: Why should people never suffer from hunger in the Sahara Desert?
Leona: I give up.
Leonard: Because of the sand which is there.

•

Leonard: If two is company and three is a crowd, what are four and five?
Leona: Who knows?
Leonard: Nine.

●

Leonard: How do you divide 19 apples equally among 13 boys if eight of the apples are small?
Leona: You've got me.
Leonard: By making applesauce.

●

Leonard: If you reached into your pants pockets and pulled out a ten-dollar bill from each pocket, what would you have?
Leona: My mind is a blank.
Leonard: Somebody else's pants on.

●

Leonard: Why did the three little pigs decide to leave home?
Leona: That's a mystery.
Leonard: They thought their father was an awful boar.

●

Leonard: What has four legs and only one foot?
Leona: I'm blank.
Leonard: A bed.

●

Leonard: What has four wheels, two horns, gives milk, and eats grass?
Leona: I don't have the foggiest.
Leonard: A cow on a skateboard.

•

Leonard: What do they call cabs lined up at the Dallas airport?
Leona: It's unknown to me.
Leonard: The yellow rows of taxis.

•

Leonard: What did Columbus first stand on when he discovered the New World?
Leona: I'm in the dark.
Leonard: His feet.

•

Leonard: If there is a red house on the right and a blue
   house on the left, where is the white house?
Leona: Search me.
Leonard: In Washington, D.C.

•

Leonard: Why did the jelly roll?
Leona: You've got me guessing.
Leonard: Because it saw the apple turnover.

Likable
Loonies

When is it safe to pet a lion?
When it's a dandelion.

•

If your loony relative was always cold, what would you
    call her?
Antifreeze.

•

When is a Chinese restaurant successful?
When it makes a fortune, cookie.

•

When does it get noisy in a magazine store?
When Time *marches on.*

•

Where do loony bunny rabbits like to spend their vacations?
On Easter Island.

•

When is a basketball player like a baby?
When he dribbles.

•

Where do pencils come from?
Pennsylvania.

•

Where should proofreaders work?
In a house of correction.

•

Where should you go if you lose your fish?
The lost-and-flounder department.

•

Where do millionaires work out?
At wealth clubs.

•

Where is one place you can always find money?
In the dictionary, of course!

•

Where do jellyfish get their jelly?
From ocean currents.

•

Where does Santa stay overnight when he travels?
At ho-ho-hotels.

•

Where do you find chili beans?
At the North Pole.

Loony League

Why do dressmakers like the wide-open spaces?
They don't feel hemmed in.

•

Why were the sardines out of work?
Because they got canned.

•

Why do tigers have stripes?
Because they would look funny in polka dots.

•

Why was the loony woman always able to remember the
names of people under five feet tall?
Because she had a short memory.

•

Why did the loon girl buy new garbage cans?
To enter the Mess America contest.

•

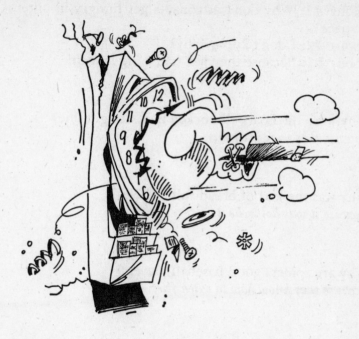

Why did the prizefighter like his new job?
He got to punch the time clock.

•

Why do you occasionally see loony people pushing a
house down the street?
That's how they jump-start their furnaces.

•

Why couldn't the loony boy see his bicycle after he
parked it behind a tree?
Because the bark was bigger than his bike.

•

Loony #1: Why don't astronauts get hungry in outer space?
Loony #2: I don't know. Why?
Loony #1: Because they just had a big launch!

•

Why were the boats all docked in a straight line?
Because they were rowboats.

•

Why was the loaf of bread full of holes?
Because it was hole wheat.

•

Why are spiders good baseball players?
Because they know how to catch flies.

•

Why did the moth eat a hole in the rug?
Because it wanted to see the floor show.

•

Why don't they make astronauts out of elephants?
Because space helmets aren't big enough to fit them.

•

Why did the hippo stop using soap?
Because he left a ring around the river.

•

Why is a schoolyard larger at recess?
Because there are more feet in it.

•

Why hasn't someone invented black light bulbs for people who want to read in the dark?

•

The loony garbageman wrote a novel. It made the best-smeller list.

•

How do you get a one-armed loony man out of a tree? *Wave.*

•

Then there was the loony football star who, when he got his varsity letter, had to have his girlfriend read it to him.

•

Loony Linda: Don't you ever peel the banana before eating it?
Loony Larry: No. I already know what's inside.

•

The Loonyville football team—nicknamed the Blockheads—no longer gets ice water. The player with the recipe graduated.

•

Did you hear about the loony man who locked his keys in the car? It took him nine hours to get his family out.

•

How do you make a loony shish kebab?
Shoot an arrow into a garbage can.

•

The loony boy was so big that he could only play seek.

•

Why did the loony man put a diaper on his clock?
Because he heard times were changing.

•

Why did the loony woman tiptoe quietly past her medicine cabinet?
Because she didn't want to wake her sleeping pills.

•

Did you hear that they had to close down the Loonyville library?
Somebody stole the book.

•

If a loony man and a loony woman jumped off a 40-story building, who would land first?
The loony man. The loony woman would have to stop and ask for directions.

•

How can you tell where a rich flamingo lives?
By the wrought-iron loonies on the front lawn.

9

Luther & Lydia Loony

Luther: What should you buy if you want to carry milk around on your wrist?
Lydia: I don't know.
Luther: A quartz watch.

•

Luther: What happens when 500 people rush to get accommodations in a hotel that has only 400 rooms?
Lydia: Beats me.
Luther: They race for space.

•

Luther: If Mother Hubbard found a frankfurter for her dog, what kind of world would it be?
Lydia: I can't guess.
Luther: A dog-eat-dog world.

•

Luther: Where does one see the handwriting on the wall?
Lydia: You tell me.
Luther: In a phone booth or a rest room.

•

Luther: What is red, has tusks, and hates to be touched?
Lydia: I have no idea.
Luther: An elephant with a sunburn.

•

Luther: What do you call a crateful of ducks?
Lydia: Who knows?
Luther: A box of quackers.

•

Luther: Where does a sheep get its hair cut?
Lydia: You've got me.
Luther: At the baa-baa shop.

•

Luther: What is the definition of a Chinese harbor?
Lydia: That's a mystery.
Luther: A junkyard.

•

Luther: What floats on the water as light as a feather, yet a thousand men can't lift it?
Lydia: I'm blank.
Luther: A bubble.

•

Luther: What comes in handy when you have a flat tire?
Lydia: I don't have the foggiest.
Luther: Despair.

Legendary Loonies

Loony visitor: Why does that old hog keep trying to come into my room? Is it because he likes me?

Loony farmer: Not really, friend. You see, that's his room during the winter.

•

Traveler in a balloon (calling down to a farmer): Ahoy there, where am I?

Loony farmer: Hah! You can't fool me, feller. You're right up there in that little basket.

•

Loony thought about short people: You're so short, you'd have to climb up on a stepladder to kick an ant in the ankle.

•

Loony mountain climber: Someone who wants to take a peak.

•

Loony boss: A man who is at work early on the days we are late.

•

Why is a calendar so popular?
Because it has lots of dates.

•

What did the loony astronomer say when he was asked what he thought about flying saucers?
"No comet."

•

Sign in a Loonyville flower shop: Love 'em and leaf 'em.

•

What do they call popcorn that is too tired to pop?
Pooped corn.

•

Did you hear about the loony student who got a real shock? He thought electricians' school was going to be easy.

•

"My business is looking better," said the loony optometrist.

•

My loony dog is so bad that last week he was expelled from obedience school.

•

Loony turtle salesman: My business is very slow.

•

Loony baker: My business is doing so well that I am rolling in the dough.

Loony teacher: Do ears of corn get dandruff?
Loony student: Sure. Haven't you ever heard of corn flakes?

•

"My business has sunk to a new low," said the loony deep-sea diver.

•

Loony Leroy: Did you hear about the poet who got arrested for writing too fast?
Loony Lester: No, what about him?
Loony Leroy: The judge took away his poetic license.

•

Loony saying: Women who use gunpowder as night cream end up with complexion that is shot.

•

Did you hear the loony radio announcer give the latest sports scores?
>The Redskins scalped the Cowboys!
>The Lions devoured the Saints!
>The Vikings butchered the Dolphins!
>The Chiefs massacred the Patriots!
>The Falcons tore the Cardinals to shreds!
>The Broncos trampled the Rams!
>The Bears mauled the Buccaneers!
>The Giants squashed the Packers!
>The Jets shot down the Eagles!
>The Bengals chewed up the Colts!

•

Loony wife: Harry, let's go jogging together.
Loony husband: Why?
Loony wife: My doctor told me I could lose weight by working out with a dumbbell.

•

"My business is sick," said the loony doctor.

•

Loony saying: Man who speak with forked tongue is
   probably a snake in the grass.

•

"My business is going up," said the loony elevator opera-
   tor.

•

A Loonyville movie star returned to his boyhood home
   for the first time since he became famous.
"I guess everyone around here talks a lot about me," the
   star said to the Loonyville mayor.
"That's right," agreed the Loonyville mayor. "You're so
   famous we even put a sign in front of your old house."
The Loonyville movie star beamed. "Really?" he ex-
   claimed. "What does the sign say?"
Smiling broadly, the Loonyville mayor replied, "It says,
   'Stop'!"

Lighthearted Loonies

What is the difference between a locomotive engineer and a schoolteacher?
One minds the train, and the other trains the mind.

•

What has four wheels and goes honk?
A goose on a skateboard.

•

What is the most boring Clark Gable film?
Yawn with the Wind.

•

What is the difference between Peter Pan and someone who quit the bomb squad?
One doesn't want to be grown up, and the other doesn't want to be blown up.

•

What do you call a man walking around with his hands in the air and waving a white flag?
A loony soldier on war maneuvers.

•

What state is the same as an unmarried woman?
Miss.

•

What snake builds things?
A boa constructor.

•

What is the difference between a crazy hare and a counterfeit coin?
One is a mad bunny, the other is bad money.

•

What does a baby snake play with?
A rattle.

•

What ride makes mothers and babies scream?
A stroller coaster.

•

What is full of holes but holds water?
A sponge.

•

What did the gingerbread man's grandfather use for walking?
A candy cane.

•

What young outlaw was very overweight?
Belly the Kid.

•

What crime-fighting gardener rides a horse and wears a
    mask?
The Lawn Ranger.

What do you get if you hit a gopher with a golf ball?
A mole-in-one.

•

What sign did the real estate agent put in front of the Old
    Woman Who Lived in a Shoe's house?
Soled.

•

What kind of bear like to bask in the sunshine?
A solar bear.

•

What is the difference between a photocopy machine
   and the Hong Kong flu?
The one makes facsimiles, the other sick families.

•

What does a maple tree like to watch on TV?
Sap operas.

•

What is a group of loony paratroopers called?
Air pollution.

•

What school do toothbrushes go to?
Colgate.

•

What do horses do for entertainment?
Watch stable TV.

•

What is a bee's favorite musical?
Stinging in the Rain.

•

What cartoon character lives in Jellystone Park and eats
   health food?
Yogurt Bear.

•

What is a dog's favorite musical?
The Hound of Music.

Leah & Lawrence Loony

Leah: How many loony psychiatrists does it take to screw in a light bulb?
Lawrence: You've got me.
Leah: Only one—but the light bulb really has to want to change.

•

Leah: What is the best way to grow fat?
Lawrence: My mind is a blank.
Leah: Raise pigs.

•

Leah: Why does the Statue of Liberty stand in New York Harbor?
Lawrence: That's a mystery.
Leah: Because it can't sit down.

•

Leah: What is another name for a nightclub?
Lawrence: I'm blank.
Leah: A rolling pin.

•

Leah: What do they call the device that keeps flies in the house?
Lawrence: I don't have the foggiest.
Leah: A window screen.

•

Leah: What makes everyone sick except those who swallow it?
Lawrence: You've got me guessing.
Leah: Flattery.

Leah: What room can no one enter?
Lawrence: I have no clue.
Leah: A mushroom.

•

Leah: What nut sounds like a sneeze?
Lawrence: It's unknown to me.
Leah: Cashew nut.

•

Leah: Where do moths dance?
Lawrence: I'm in the dark.
Leah: At a mothball.

•

Leah: When does 10 plus 7 equal 13?
Lawrence: Search me.
Leah: When you add wrong.

•

Leah: What kind of fish do dogs like to chase?
Lawrence: I pass.
Leah: Catfish.

•

Leah: Where does the Lone Ranger take his garbage?
Lawrence: How should I know?
Leah: To the dump, to the dump, to the dump, dump, dump.

•

Leah: How do batteries get sick?
Lawrence: I don't know.
Leah: They get acid indigestion.

•

Leah: How do you become a coroner?
Lawrence: I don't know.
Leah: You have to take a stiff examination.

•

Leah: What is round and dangerous?
Lawrence: Beats me.
Leah: A vicious circle.

Loony Laughter

The biggest social event of the season at the Loony Pen Manufacturing Company is the "Pen Point Ball."

•

Loony #1: Did you hear about the dog that went to the flea circus?
Loony #2: No. What happened?
Loony #1: He stole the show.

•

I work only when I'm fired. What am I?
A rocket.

•

It's funny, but a loony horse eats best when it doesn't have a bit in its mouth.

•

Larry Loony: My brother swallowed a box of firecrackers.
Louis Loony: Is he all right now?
Larry Loony: I don't know. We haven't heard the last report.

•

Loony lima bean: I had a date with a green bean, but I
     think she only went out with me because of the money
     I spent on her.
Loony pork 'n' bean: I think she's stringing you along.

•

Who screams "The sky is falling! The sky is falling!" and
     suffers from inflation?
Henny Nickel.

•

I have wings, but I can't fly. What am I?
A large mansion.

•

I have teeth, but no mouth. What am I?
A comb.

•

I have hands and a face, but I can't touch or smile. What
     am I?
A clock.

•

I have legs, but I can't walk. What am I?
A chair.

•

That guy is so frail and skinny that the last time someone
     kicked sand in his face, the grains knocked him out
     cold.

•

Loony #1: Are there any fish that are musical?
Loony #2: Of course! Didn't you ever hear of a piano tuna?

•

I lived in a tough Loonyville neighborhood. On Christmas
Eve I hung my stockings over the fireplace, and Santa
Claus stole them.

•

I know a loony man who is so dumb, the only thing that
can stay in his head for more than a day is a cold.

•

Loony #1: Wow! You are dumb. In fact, you are the closest thing to an idiot.
Loony #2: Want me to move away from you?

•

Little Laura Loony was visiting her grandmother on the farm for the first time. One day she spotted a peacock, a bird she had never seen before. She stared at it silently for a few moments, then ran into the house crying, "Oh, Granny, come look! One of your chickens is blooming!"

•

What do they call a loony hobo who has been caught in a pouring rain?
A damp tramp.

•

We have only two loony things to worry about—one, that things will never get back to normal, and two, that they already have.

•

He is so loony that if his looniness was gold, he would be Fort Knox.

•

My loony friend is such a lazy person that waking him up in the morning makes him tired.

•

Did you hear about the loony upside-down lighthouse?
It's for submarines.

•

Did you hear about the loony skin diver who failed divers'
school? The subjects were just too deep for him.

Loony Knock-Knock Jokes

Knock, knock.
Who's there?
Chester.
Chester who?
Chester minute and I'll see.

•

Knock, knock.
Who's there?
Desdemona.
Desdemona who?
Desdemona Lisa still hang on the gallery wall?

●

Knock, knock.
Who's there?
Jewel.
Jewel who?
Jewel know who when you open the door.

●

Knock, knock.
Who's there?
Anita Loos.
Anita Loos who?
Anita Loos about 20 pounds.

●

Knock, knock.
Who's there?
Ghana.
Ghana who?
Ghana wash that man right out of my hair.

●

Knock, knock.
Who's there?
Gil.
Gil who?
Gil the umpire!

●

Will you remember me in five years?
Yes.
Will you remember me next year?
Yes.
Will you remember me next month?
Yes.
Will you remember me next week?
Yes.
Will you remember me tomorrow?
Yes.
Will you remember me in another minute?
Yes.
Will you remember me in another second?
Yes.
Knock, knock.
Who's there?
You forgot me already?

•

Knock, knock.
Who's there?
Dawn.
Dawn who?
Dawnkey. Hee-haw.

•

Knock, knock.
Who's there?
Uganda.
Uganda who?
Uganda come in without knocking!

Laurel & LaVonne
Loony

Laurel: What should you do if you feel strongly about graffiti?
LaVonne: I'm in the dark.
Laurel: Sign a partition.

•

Laurel: Where does a bird go when it's ill?
LaVonne: Search me.
Laurel: It goes for tweetment.

•

Laurel: What is the difference between a shoe that hurts your foot and an oak tree?
LaVonne: You've got me guessing.
Laurel: One makes corns ache, the other makes acorns.

•

Laurel: What is the name for an older person who keeps your mother from spanking you?
LaVonne: I pass.
Laurel: A grandparent.

•

Laurel: Why are loony writers the strangest creatures in the world?
LaVonne: How should I know?
Laurel: Because their tales come out of their heads.

•

Laurel: Why would a compliment from a chicken be an insult?
LaVonne: I don't know.
Laurel: Because it's a fowl remark.

•

Laurel: What do they call a boxer who gets beat up in a fight?
LaVonne: I have no clue.
Laurel: A sore loser.

•

Laurel: What did Mrs. Bullet say to Mr. Bullet?
LaVonne: I don't know.
Laurel: Darling, I'm going to have a BB!

•

Laurel: Which is the largest room in the world?
LaVonne: Beats me.
Laurel: The room for improvement.

•

Laurel: Where do Eskimos keep their money?
LaVonne: I can't guess.
Laurel: In a snowbank.

•

Laurel: How many balls of string would it take to reach to
the moon?
LaVonne: I have no idea.
Laurel: One, if it was long enough.

•

Laurel: Which day is stronger, Sunday or Monday?
LaVonne: You tell me.
Laurel: Sunday is stronger. Monday is a weekday.

•

Laurel: What is always behind time?
LaVonne: I give up.
Laurel: The back of a watch.

•

Laurel: What question can never be answered by saying yes?
LaVonne: Beats me.
Laurel: Are you asleep?

Loony Lampoon

Who was born on a mountaintop, killed a bear when he was only three, and swims underwater?
Davy Crocodile.

•

Who got nervous picking pickled peppers?
P-P-P-P-P-Peter P-P-P-P-P-Piper.

•

Who is short, can spin gold from straw, and is very, very wrinkled?
Crumplestiltskin.

•

Who caught flies with his tongue and was the first treasurer of the United States?
Salamander Hamilton.

•

Who writes mystery stories and blooms in spring?
Edgar Allan Poe-sy.

•

Who trains court jesters?
Fool teachers.

•

Whom do mice see when they get sick?
The Hickory Dickory Doc.

How do you make a hot dog stand?
Steal its chair.

•

How did the loony musician break his leg?
He fell over a clef.

•

How does a loony farmer mend his overalls?
With cabbage patches.

•

How did the mouse pass his final exam?
He just squeaked by.

•

How did Noah know how to build an ark?
He studied archaeology!

•

Loony #1: How are you doing with your wood carving?
Loony #2: It's coming along whittle by whittle.

•

How does an elephant get out of a Volkswagen?
The same way it got in.

Loony Students

Loony student: Teacher, is there life after death?
Teacher: Why do you ask?
Loony student: I may need the extra time to finish all this homework you gave us.

•

Teacher: Everyone knows we should conserve energy. Larry, name one way we can do that.
Loony Larry: By staying in bed all day.

•

Teacher: Lacey, how many books did you finish over the summer?
Loony Lacey: None. My brother stole my box of crayons.

•

Teacher: When did George Washington die?
Loony Lester: It was just a few days before they buried him.

•

Teacher: Leena, what is the first thing you should do with a barrel of crude oil?
Loony Leena: Teach it some manners.

•

Teacher: Why should we never use the word "ain't"?
Loony Leroy: Because it ain't correct.

•

Teacher: Where do we find the Suez Canal?
Loony Leslie: It should be written right here on my sleeve with the rest of the answers.

Lynette & LeRoy Loony

Lynette: How many peas in a pint?
LeRoy: I don't know.
Lynette: One.

•

Lynette: What makes more noise than a cat howling at midnight?
LeRoy: I'm in the dark.
Lynette: Two cats howling at midnight.

•

Lynette: What kind of bird do you find in your throat?
LeRoy: Search me.
Lynette: A swallow.

•

Lynette: What is another name people give to their mistakes?
LeRoy: I pass.
Lynette: Experience.

•

Lynette: What do you call a newborn beetle?
LeRoy: You've got me guessing.
Lynette: A baby buggy!

•

Lynette: Why is it hard to drive a golf ball?
LeRoy: How should I know?
Lynette: It doesn't have a steering wheel.

•

Lynette: What is the difference between one lawyer in a
    small town and two lawyers in a small town?
LeRoy: I have no clue.
Lynette: One can earn an okay living, but two can make a
    fortune.

•

Lynette: What kind of doctor would a duck make?
LeRoy: I don't know.
Lynette: A quack doctor.

•

Lynette: What do you call it when your teacher phones
your parents to tell them how poorly you're doing in
school?
LeRoy: I don't know.
Lynette: A bad connection.

•

Lynette: Where is the Secretary of State's chair?
LeRoy: Beats me.
Lynette: Undersecretary of State.

•

Lynette: What kind of seafood makes a good sandwich?
LeRoy: I can't guess.
Lynette: Jellyfish.

•

Lynette: What is the best thing to do for that run-down
feeling?
LeRoy: I have no idea.
Lynette: Get the license number of the car.

•

Lynette: Which state produces the most marriages?
LeRoy: I give up.
Lynette: The state of matrimony.

•

Lynette: Why does a little boy look one way and then the other way before crossing the street?

LeRoy: You tell me.

Lynette: Because he can't look both ways at the same time.

19

Lovable Loonies

If tires hold up cars, what holds up an airplane?
Hijackers!

•

What state is like a father?
Pa.

•

What state was important to Noah?
Ark.

•

What state is like a piece of clothing?
New Jersey.

•

What is a cat's favorite side dish at lunch?
Mice-aroni and cheese.

•

What is black, covered with feathers, and weighs 2,000 pounds?
An elephant that has been tarred and feathered.

•

What is gray and stamps out jungle fires?
Smokey Elephant.

•

What is the worst flower to invite to a party?
A daffo-dull.

•

What is the difference between Christopher Columbus and the lid of a dish?
One is a discoverer; the other is a dish coverer.

•

What do you get when you cross an owl with an oyster?
An animal that drops pearls of wisdom.

•

What mouse heads the House of Representatives?
The Squeaker of the House.

•

What U.S. president got hit by a truck?
George Squashington.

•

What do you need to spot an iceberg 20 miles away?
Good ice sight.

•

What do you get if you drop Limburger cheese in the
toaster?
You get out of the kitchen as fast as you can.

•

What would you get if you crossed an alligator with a
pickle?
A crocodill.

•

What do you call two convicts who become buddies in jail?
Pen pals.

•

What occurs once in a minute, twice in a moment, but not once in a hundred years?
The letter m.

•

What is the difference between an 11-year-old girl and a 15-year-old girl?
A $5 difference in your phone bill.

•

What did Adam say on the day before Christmas?
It's Christmas, Eve.

•

What is the difference between a lollipop and a chicken?
One you suck and one you pluck.

•

What do you give an elk with indigestion?
Elk-A-Seltzer.

•

What should you do if you find yourself with water on the knee, water on the elbow, and water on the brain?
Turn off the shower.

•

What happens when the sun gets tired?
It sets awhile.

•

What kind of teeth can you buy for a dollar?
Buck teeth.

•

What ice cream do monkeys eat?
Chocolate chimp.

Loony
Doctors

Patient: Doctor, my child just swallowed a pen. What should I do?
Loony doctor: Use a pencil.

•

Patient: Doctor, you've gotta do something for me. I snore so loudly that I wake myself up.
Loony doctor: In that case, sleep in another room.

•

Patient: Doctor, what's the difference between an itch and an allergy?
Loony doctor: About $35.

•

Patient: Doctor, nobody can figure out what is wrong with me. I've got the oddest collection of symptoms.
Loony doctor: Have you had it before?
Patient: Yes.
Loony doctor: Well, you've got it again.

•

Patient: Doctor, every bone in my body hurts.
Loony doctor: Be glad you're not a herring.

•

Patient: Doctor, what am I really allergic to?
Loony doctor: Paying my bills.

•

Nurse: Doctor, I just wanted to let you know that there is
   an invisible man in your waiting room.
Loony doctor: Tell him I can't see him now.

•

Patient: Doctor, my child just swallowed a dozen aspirin.
   What should I do?
Loony doctor: Give him a headache.

•

Patient: Doctor, there's something wrong with my stomach.
Loony doctor: Keep your coat buttoned and nobody will
   notice it.

•

Patient: Doctor, is it a boy?
Loony doctor: Well, the one in the middle is.

•

Did you hear about the loony dentist who thought he had
   a lot of pull?

•

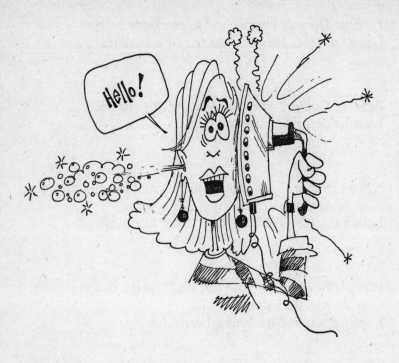

Doctor: I've never seen anything quite like these second-degree burns on both your ears. How did you get them?

Loony Loretta: Well, the phone rang and I picked up the steam iron by mistake.

Doctor: But what about the other ear?

Loony Loretta: They called back.

•

Patient: Doctor, I think everyone tries to take advantage of me.

Loony psychiatrist: Don't worry. That's a perfectly normal feeling.

Patient: Is it really? Thanks for your help, doctor. How much do I owe you?

Loony psychiatrist: How much do you have?

Lila & Lillian
Loony

Lila: What color is a hiccup?
Lillian: I pass.
Lila: Burple.

•

Lila: What is the longest sentence in the world?
Lillian: How should I know?
Lila: Life in prison.

•

Lila: Why is the stork associated with birth?
Lillian: I don't know.
Lila: Because we all come into this world stork naked.

•

Lila: What do they call a textbook wired for sound?
Lillian: I have no clue.
Lila: A professor.

•

Lila: What would you call a gold digger?
Lillian: Beats me.
Lila: A human gimmee pig.

•

Lila: What did one volcano say to the other volcano?
Lillian: Who knows?
Lila: I lava you.

•

Lila: What is a bore?
Lillian: I don't know.
Lila: A person who can change the topic of a conversation faster than you can change it back to yours.

•

Lila: How should you refer to a tailor when you don't remember his name?
Lillian: I can't guess.
Lila: As Mr. So-and-So.

•

Lila: What falls often but never gets hurt?
Lillian: I have no idea.
Lila: Rain.

●

Lila: What is another name for coffee?
Lillian: I give up.
Lila: Break fluid.

●

Lila: What do you say when you call your dog and he doesn't come?
Lillian: You've got me.
Lila: Doggone!

●

Lila: What should you do when your nick is ripe?
Lillian: My mind is a blank.
Lila: Picnic.

●

Lila: What do you have when you were planning to serve strawberries and cake and you forgot to buy the cake?
Lillian: That's a mystery.
Lila: Strawberry shortcake.

Loony Definitions

Acquaintance: A person you know well enough to borrow money from, but not well enough to lend money to.

•

Airplanes: The world's leading cause of white knuckles.

•

Amiss: Someone who is not married.

•

Blind date: When you expect to meet a vision, and she turns out to be a sight.

•

Bore: A person who insists upon talking about himself when you want to talk about yourself.

•

Boredom: A state of mind that usually ends when school lets out.

•

Childish games: Those at which your spouse beats you.

•

Cost plus: Expensive.

•

Claustrophobia: Fear of Santa.

•

Dogsled: Polar coaster.

•

Flood: A river too big for its bridges.

•

Flashlight: A case to carry dead batteries in.

•

Gossip: Good memory with a tongue hung in the middle of it.

•

Highborn: Anybody born on top of a mountain.

●

Iceberg: A kind of permanent wave.

●

Little Leaguer: Peanut batter.

●

Peanut butter: A bread spread.

●

Stationery store: A store that stays pretty much at the same location.

●

Trapeze artist: A guy who gets the hang of things.

●

Traffic light: A little green light that changes to red as your car approaches.

●

Zoo: A place where animals look at silly people.

Loony
Waiters

Diner: Waiter, I'm in a hurry. Will the griddle cakes be
  long?
Loony waiter: No, sir. They'll all be round.

•

Diner: Waiter, this steak is rare. Didn't you hear me say "well done"?

Loony waiter: Yes, sir. Thank you, sir!

•

Diner: Do you have lobster tails?

Loony waiter: Certainly, sir: Once upon a time, there was a little lobster...

•

Diner: Waiter, there's a fly in my soup!

Loony waiter: That's funny. There were two of them when I left the kitchen.

•

Diner: Waiter, isn't this toast burned?

Loony waiter: No, sir. It just fell on the floor.

•

Diner: Waiter, there's a fly in my soup!

Loony waiter: Don't worry. The frog should snap it up any second now.

•

Diner: Waiter, do you serve crabs here?

Loony waiter: We serve anyone; sit down.

Lois & Lola
Loony

Lois: What is the best thing to do if you are going to be
   beheaded?
Lola: I don't have the foggiest.
Lois: Stay calm and try not to lose your head.

•

Lois: What goes ha-ha-ha-plop?
Lola: It's unknown to me.
Lois: Someone who laughs his head off.

•

Lois: Where does a pig go to pawn his watch?
Lola: I'm in the dark.
Lois: He goes to a ham hock shop.

•

Lois: Why is a wig like a lie?
Lola: Search me.
Lois: Because it's a falsehood.

•

Lois: Which animal keeps the best time?
Lola: I'm blank.
Lois: A watchdog.

•

Lois: What should you do to keep from getting sick the
    night before a trip?
Lola: You've got me guessing.
Lois: Leave a day earlier.

•

Lois: What kind of clothing lasts the longest?
Lola: I pass.
Lois: Underwear, because it is never worn out.

•

Lois: What can you make that you can't see?
Lola: How should I know?
Lois: Noise.

•

Lois: Why do giraffes find it difficult to apologize?
Lola: I don't know.
Lois: It takes them a long time to swallow their pride.

•

Lois: What do you call a frightened skin diver?
Lola: I have no clue.
Lois: Chicken of the sea.

•

Lois: What kind of saw lives in the sea?
Lola: Beats me.
Lois: A seesaw.

•

Lois: What is an anonymous story?
Lola: I can't guess.
Lois: Unauthorized.

•

Lois: What shall we do if Amos acts silly?
Lola: I have no idea.
Lois: Ignoramus.

More Loony Knock-Knock Jokes

Knock, knock.
Who's there?
Amarillo.
Amarillo who?
Amarillo-fashioned cowboy.

•

Knock, knock.
Who's there?
Eskimo, Christian, Italian.
Eskimo, Christian, Italian who?
Eskimo, Christian, Italian no lies.
  (Ask me no questions; I'll tell you no lies.)

•

Knock, knock.
Who's there?
Alby.
Alby who?
Alby glad when school is over.

•

Knock, knock.
Who's there?
Duncan.
Duncan who?
Duncan doughnuts in your milk makes 'em soft.

•

Knock, knock.
Who's there?
Amos.
Amos who?
Amos-kito bit me.

•

Knock, knock.
Who's there?
Andy.
Andy who?
Andy bit me again.

•

Knock, knock.
Who's there?
Apollo.
Apollo who?
Apollo you anywhere if you'll blow in my ear.

•

Knock, knock.
Who's there?
Sari.
Sari who?
Sari I was sarong!

•

Knock, knock.
Who's there?
Ether.
Ether who?
Ether Bunny.

Knock, knock.
Who's there?
Stella.
Stella who?
Stella nother Ether Bunny.

Knock, knock.
Who's there?
Samoa.
Samoa who?
Samoa Ether Bunnies.

Luann & Lowell
Loony

Luann: What is the surest way to keep water from coming into your house?
Lowell: You tell me.
Luann: Don't pay your water bill.

•

Luann: Who is married to an Egyptian daddy?
Lowell: I give up.
Luann: An Egyptian mummy.

•

Luann: What remedy is there for someone who splits his sides with laughter?
Lowell: Who knows?
Luann: Have him run as fast as he can...till he gets a stitch in his side.

•

Luann: What is the best thing to put into cake?
Lowell: My mind is a blank.
Luann: Your teeth.

•

Luann: How do you make an elephant float?
Lowell: I don't have the foggiest.
Luann: Put him and two scoops of ice cream into a glass
   of soda.

•

Luann: What did the mayonnaise say to the refrigerator?
Lowell: That's a mystery.
Luann: Shut the door. I'm dressing.

•

Luann: Which eats more grass—black sheep or white?
Lowell: I'm blank.
Luann: White, because there are more of them.

•

Luann: What word is always pronounced wrong?
Lowell: You've got me.
Luann: Wrong.

•

Luann: What is the best weather for gathering hay?
Lowell: I'm in the dark.
Luann: When it rains pitchforks.

•

Luann: What does not break no matter how far it falls?
Lowell: Search me.
Luann: A leaf.

Luann: How do you communicate with a fish?
Lowell: How should I know?
Luann: Drop it a line.

•

Luann: Why isn't your ear 12 inches long?
Lowell: You've got me guessing.
Luann: If it were, it would be a foot.

•

Luann: What is a cannibal?
Lowell: I pass.
Luann: Someone who is fed up with people.

•

Luann: Why is it dangerous for farmers to plant peas
   during a war?
Lowell: I don't know.
Luann: The enemy might come along and shell them.

Other Books by Bob Phillips

- *World's Greatest Collection of Clean Jokes*
- *More Good Clean Jokes*
- *The Last of the Good Clean Jokes*
- *The Return of the Good Clean Jokes*
- *The All American Joke Book*
- *The World's Greatest Collection of Heavenly Humor*
- *The Best of the Good Clean Jokes*
- *The Best of the Good Clean Jokes Perpetual Calendar*
- *Wit and Wisdom*
- *Humor Is Tremendous*
- *The All-New Clean Joke Book*
- *Good Clean Jokes for Kids*
- *The Encyclopedia of Good Clean Jokes*
- *Ultimate Good Clean Jokes for Kids*
- *Awesome Good Clean Jokes For Kids*
- *Wacky Good Clean Jokes For Kids*
- *Bible Brainteasers*
- *The Ultimate Bible Trivia Challenge*
- *The Little Book of Bible Trivia*
- *How Can I Be Sure? A Pre-Marriage Inventory*
- *Anger Is a Choice*
- *Redi-Reference*
- *Redi-Reference Daily Bible Reading Plan*
- *The Delicate Art of Dancing with Porcupines*
- *Powerful Thinking for Powerful Living*
- *God's Hand Over Hume*
- *Praise Is a Three-Lettered Word—Joy*
- *The Handbook for Headache Relief*
- *Friendship, Love & Laughter*

For information on how to purchase any of the above books, contact your local bookstore or send a self-addressed stamped envelope to:

Family Services
P.O. Box 9363
Fresno, CA 93702

Dear Reader:

We would appreciate hearing from you regarding this Harvest House book. It will enable us to continue to give you the best in Christian publishing.

1. What most influenced you to purchase *Loony Good Clean Jokes for Kids*?
   - ☐ Author
   - ☐ Subject matter
   - ☐ Backcover copy
   - ☐ Recommendations
   - ☐ Cover/Title
   - ☐ _____

2. Where did you purchase this book?
   - ☐ Christian bookstore
   - ☐ General bookstore
   - ☐ Department store
   - ☐ Grocery store
   - ☐ Other

3. Your overall rating of this book:
   - ☐ Excellent   ☐ Very good   ☐ Good   ☐ Fair   ☐ Poor

4. How likely would you be to purchase other books by this author?
   - ☐ Very likely
   - ☐ Somewhat likely
   - ☐ Not very likely
   - ☐ Not at all

5. What types of books most interest you?
   (check all that apply)
   - ☐ Women's Books
   - ☐ Marriage Books
   - ☐ Current Issues
   - ☐ Self Help/Psychology
   - ☐ Bible Studies
   - ☐ Fiction
   - ☐ Biographies
   - ☐ Children's Books
   - ☐ Youth Books
   - ☐ Other _____

6. Please check the box next to your age group.
   - ☐ Under 18
   - ☐ 18-24
   - ☐ 25-34
   - ☐ 35-44
   - ☐ 45-54
   - ☐ 55 and over

Mail to: Editorial Director
Harvest House Publishers
1075 Arrowsmith
Eugene, OR 97402

Name _____

Address _____

City _____ State _____ Zip _____

**Thank you for helping us to help you
in future publications!**